My First Bible and Prayers

Cover illustrated by Emily Dove
Illustrated by Charlotte Cooke, Iris Deppe, Emily Dove,
Chiara Fiorentino, John Joven, Xuan Le, Tiziana Longo, Madison Mastrangelo,
Alessandra Psacharopulo, Laura Rigo, Luisa Uribe, and Ben Whitehouse

Bible stories retold by Rachel Moss and Catherine Allison
Additional prayers by Meryl Doney and Jan Payne

Every effort has been made to acknowledge the contributors to this book.
If we have made any errors, we will be pleased to rectify them in future editions.

First published 2016 by Parragon Books, Ltd.
Copyright © 2018 Cottage Door Press, LLC
5005 Newport Drive, Rolling Meadows, Illinois 60008
All Rights Reserved

ISBN 978-1-68052-408-6

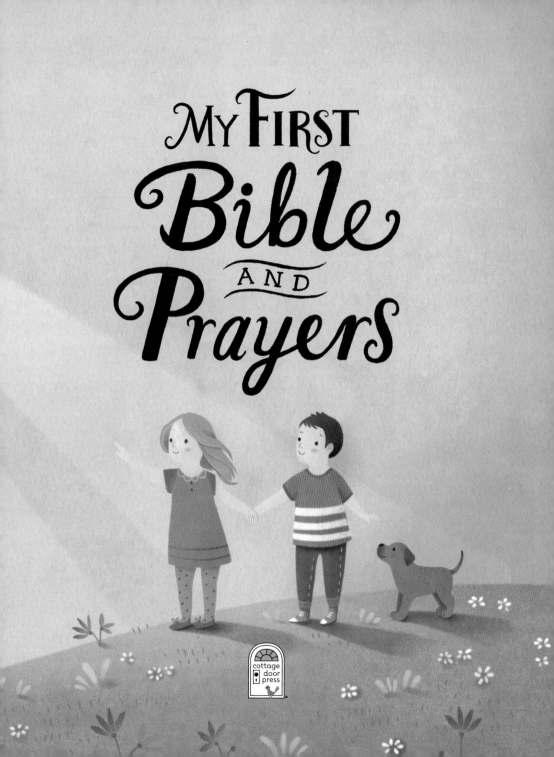

My First Bible AND Prayers

cottage door press

Contents

The Old Testament

10
The Creation Story
ILLUSTRATED BY MADISON MASTRANGELO

34
Noah's Ark
ILLUSTRATED BY IRIS DEPPE

58
The Tower of Babel
ILLUSTRATED BY TIZIANA LONGO

60
Abraham and Sarah
ILLUSTRATED BY TIZIANA LONGO

62
Jacob and Esau
ILLUSTRATED BY TIZIANA LONGO

66
Joseph and His Coat of Many Colors
ILLUSTRATED BY JOHN JOVEN

90

Moses

ILLUSTRATED BY TIZIANA LONGO

94

Moses and the Israelites

ILLUSTRATED BY LAURA RIGO

98

The Israelites Conquer Jericho

ILLUSTRATED BY TIZIANA LONGO

100

The First King of Israel

ILLUSTRATED BY TIZIANA LONGO

104

David and Goliath

ILLUSTRATED BY LAURA RIGO

108

King Solomon

ILLUSTRATED BY TIZIANA LONGO

110

Daniel and the Lions

ILLUSTRATED BY TIZIANA LONGO

114

Jonah and the Whale

ILLUSTRATED BY XUAN LE

The New Testament

140
The Christmas Story
ILLUSTRATED BY LUISA URIBE

164
Jesus Visits the Temple
ILLUSTRATED BY TIZIANA LONGO

166
Jesus Is Baptized
ILLUSTRATED BY TIZIANA LONGO

168
Jesus and His Disciples
ILLUSTRATED BY TIZIANA LONGO

170
Jesus Feeds 5,000 People
ILLUSTRATED BY LAURA RIGO

172
Jesus Walks on Water
ILLUSTRATED BY LAURA RIGO

174
The Easter Story
ILLUSTRATED BY XUAN LE

Prayers

200
My World Is Wonderful
ILLUSTRATED BY EMILY DOVE

308
Help Me to Be Good
ILLUSTRATED BY ALESSANDRA PSACHAROPULO

234
God Bless the Animals
ILLUSTRATED BY LUISA URIBE

328
It's a Special Day
ILLUSTRATED BY MADISON MASTRANGELO

260
Thank You for My Food
ILLUSTRATED BY CHIARA FIORENTINO

352
Now I'm Going to Sleep
ILLUSTRATED BY CHARLOTTE COOKE

286
Look After My Family
ILLUSTRATED BY BEN WHITEHOUSE

The Old Testament

The Creation Story

In the beginning, before time began, there was nothing. Nothing to see. Nothing to hear. Nothing to touch or smell. There was only silence. God moved alone through the inky darkness.

Then God created the heavens and the Earth, and the Earth
was covered by water.

"Let there be light," God said.

It was faint at first, a flicker in the darkness that grew and grew.
It became a glowing ball that pushed the gloom aside, soft and
yellow, then red, pink, and dazzling gold.

God delighted in its loveliness. The changing light seemed
to have a life of its own, and God called it "day." When the light
faded into darkness, He named it "night."

It was the very first day of the world.

On the second day, when the light came back,
God made the sky. It was a soft, bright blue, and it
hung over the Earth like a canopy.

On the third day of the world, God drew back the choppy waters, so that solid ground appeared. The great pools of water, blue like the sky and shimmering in the light, He named "seas." He called the big, muddy areas of ground "land."

The land was flat and bare, so God shaped it into mountains, plains, and deep valleys. Under His guiding hand, greenery covered the Earth. Grasses and plants of every size, shape, and color took root; sweet-smelling flowers blossomed; sticky buds opened; and vines coiled upward.

Trees sprang from the ground, their branches reaching for the sky, growing tall and heavy with fruit. The Earth had become lush and green, and brimmed with plant life.

On the fourth day, God said, "Let there be signs to mark the day and night."

He made the fiery Sun to show the day and the gentle Moon to shine at night. During the day, the Moon hid in the shadows. At night, the Sun turned its golden face away, while the Moon cast its silvery beams over the land.

God also brightened the night sky with millions upon millions of tiny glittering stars. He felt pleased with the beautiful world He had created.

God's new world was a peaceful land filled with flowers, trees, and rushing rivers, but there were no birds to perch in the trees. There were no bees to buzz from flower to flower, nor fish to leap through the waves. The only sounds were the whisper of the wind among the leaves and the waves lapping the shores.

On the fifth day, God filled the waters with living creatures. Suddenly, the sea teemed with fish that moved as one. He made whales that sent great plumes of spray high up into the sky and dolphins that leaped playfully in and out of the waves.

He made jellyfish that shimmered like
moonlight, shellfish that sparkled like precious
stones, and tiny crabs that waved their claws
on the golden sands.

Then God said, "Let there be creatures of the air that will fill the sky with life."

There began a great fluttering of feathers and flapping of wings, and a cloud of birds and insects of all shapes and sizes rose into the sky. Tiny chirruping sparrows mingled with colorful parakeets and silent, gliding hawks. The sky was alive with color and sound as the twittering birds found shelter among the trees and bushes, discovered fruit, and washed their feathers in the bright streams. Their happy songs filled God's ears, and He blessed them.

On the sixth day of the world, God said, "Now, let there be creatures on the land!" and the Earth began to shake with the thunder of a thousand feet.

The world hummed with voices large and small, jostling to be heard. Regal lions prowled beside mighty elephants and rhinos. Monkeys swung through the trees, cackling to each other, and bears lumbered through the undergrowth.

Fierce animals paced side by side with the gentlest of God's creatures. Everyone, from the tiny shrews to the tall giraffes, was looking for a new home. Some liked the cool of the snowy mountains, and some preferred the heat of the rain forests. Snakes slithered into the jungles, crocodiles hid in rivers, and squirrels climbed tall trees. The world was pulsing with life.

God looked around and was happy with what He saw.
But something was missing.

"Who will care for all the animals?" God asked Himself.

He took handfuls of earth and shaped a creature who looked like Him. He breathed life into him and called him "man." Then he took a rib from the man. With the rib, God created "woman." The man and woman opened their eyes and stared around them in wonder. Slowly, they stretched their arms and legs, and rose to their feet. They stood in front of God, holding hands, as beautiful and innocent as the new world.

God blessed them, and named the man Adam and the woman Eve.

"Your job is to look after the wonders I have created," He said. "You will rule over the fish in the sea, the birds in the sky, and every creature on the Earth. You will have fruit to eat and water to drink. I want you to enjoy your life here."

God's work was done. The world was every bit as beautiful as He had imagined.

It was the seventh day, and God rested.

Next, God made a beautiful garden for Adam and Eve, and named it Eden. There were flowers, and trees full of delicious fruit to eat, and velvet-soft grass to lie on. A sparkling stream gave Adam and Eve clean water to drink.

There was a huge tree in the middle of the garden. Its branches reached into the sky like upstretched arms, and God named it the Tree of Knowledge.

"You can pick fruit from any tree in the garden, except the Tree of Knowledge," He told Adam and Eve. "If you eat from that tree, you will die."

Adam and Eve listened to everything God told them. They had all that they needed and they were happy. They cared for the animals and the garden, just as God had told them.

One day, Eve was picking berries near the Tree of Knowledge when she heard rustling in the leaves of the tree. A snake was watching her, its tongue flicking in and out.

"Sssmell the sssweet fruit," the snake hissed. "Try it. Tassste it!"

"No," Eve replied. "God has told us we must not eat the fruit from the Tree of Knowledge or we will die."

The snake shook its head. "It would make you as wissse as God," it said. "Jussst one bite would make you a goddessss."

The snake's words made
Eve long to try it. Slowly, she
plucked a ripe fruit and drew it
toward her. It smelled sweet and
delicious. Her heart thumped
with fear and excitement.

Eve could not resist. She took a tiny bite of the fruit. Adam saw her and, although he knew that it was wrong, he burned with curiosity. So Eve handed him the fruit and he tried it. Smiling, the snake slithered away.

God knew at once what Adam and Eve had done. He was upset and angry.

"You must leave Eden," He told them. "From now on, the lives of humankind will be full of trouble and worry. Now that you have eaten from the Tree of Knowledge, your bodies will eventually die. But I will find a way to save you."

Adam and Eve shivered and wept as they left Eden behind them. Greed had taken them from a place of gentle breezes to a cruel world where the wind bit and the rain soaked their bodies.

But God, who loves His people, gave Adam and Eve something very special. He gave them hope. Perhaps one day, He told them, humankind might yet return to the beautiful garden of Eden and to the love of God.

Noah's Ark

Long, long ago, when the world was still new, God saw that all was not well. Golden sun still warmed the days on Earth, silver moonlight gilded the nights, and the hills, valleys, rivers, and seas were as beautiful as on the day God made them. But the world had changed. The people had become wicked. They fought one another, hurt one another, and made mischief. They had forgotten that God wanted them to be good—in fact, they had forgotten God completely. Seeing this made God so unhappy that He wished He'd never made people. He decided that something must be done.

As God looked down on the world, His eyes fell upon one man, whose name was Noah. Noah was the only man on Earth who remembered God. He worked hard every day, despite the fact that he was very old. His wife, his three sons, and his sons' wives all worked hard, too. They were happy, kind to each other, and good to their neighbors, even though they received no kindness in return. They lived a good life—the sort of life God had hoped all people would live when He created them.

God was pleased with Noah and his family. He decided that they deserved to live on Earth and He would protect them. But everyone else had been wicked, and they could not be saved.

God told Noah about His plan to
change the world.

"The world is full of wickedness,"
God said, "so I am going to send
a great flood to wash it clean.
Nearly everyone and everything
will be wiped away, apart from
you and your family, Noah.
The world will begin again,
as fresh and good as when
it was first created, and you and
your family will live there."

Noah was very frightened.

"What must I do?" he
asked, trembling.

"You should build an ark,"
said God. "It must be big enough to
hold two of every animal in the world—
one male and one female—and food for all
of them. It must be strong and watertight,
because it will be battered by the flood
waters for many days."

"I will do exactly as you say,"
said Noah.

Extra-strong shutters

2 cubits

Tall room for giraffes

Cold area for penguins or seals

Pandas

Lions or tigers

Zebras

Stairway 2 plus storage

More storage

Walruses

Rope for monkey

Noah was glad that he and his family would be saved from the flood, but he was sad about what would happen to the world and all the other people, and worried about what God had told him to do.

"How can I build such an ark? I'm not a shipbuilder," he thought. "And how can I collect so many animals? God expects so much of me and I'm afraid I will fail."

But God wouldn't let Noah fail. He was there beside Noah every step of the way, helping him and telling him what to do.

Noah and his sons worked hard, chopping, sawing, sanding, and hammering, and gradually the ark took shape.

While Noah worked, God spoke to him.

"It will rain for forty days and forty nights, and the land will be covered with water. But you, Noah, will be safe in the ark."

As Noah and his sons worked, their neighbors watched from a distance.

"What are you doing, Noah?" they asked, laughing at him. "Why do you need a boat when the sea is miles away?"

Noah heard them laughing, but he took no notice.

After many weeks, the ark was finished. It was taller, longer, and stronger than any boat there had ever been. It was slick, smooth, and shiny on the outside, with strong shutters at the windows and heavy locks on the door—the perfect boat for stormy weather. Inside, there were many rooms, some wide enough for the largest pair of elephants to walk side by side, others high enough for the tallest giraffes to stand in without bending their necks.

All of a sudden, dark clouds appeared in the sky and thunder
rumbled. The people who had been laughing at Noah saw that
the weather was changing and started to head for home.

Noah's Ark

"Perhaps Noah isn't such a fool after all," said one. "There's a storm coming for sure, and he'll be safe and dry inside the ark."

Noah began to gather the animals—a male and a female of every creature that hopped, walked, crawled, or flew on Earth. There were cats, bats, and rats, monkeys and donkeys, hooting owls and wolves that howled, big baboons and little raccoons— so many animals, of all shapes and sizes. Noah and his sons gently led the animals up the gangplank and into the ark as the rain began to fall.

"We don't have much time," thought Noah.

The sky turned black and the rain fell harder. Noah's wife, his sons, and his sons' wives made sure all the animals were safely on board, then they went into the ark. With one last glance at the world he loved, Noah went inside, too, and shut the heavy door behind him.

Noah's Ark

Outside the ark, rain fell everywhere. Not a soft drizzle, but soak-to-the-skin, drench-to-the-bone rain. Raindrops became puddles, and puddles flowed into streams, oozed into lakes, and poured into wild rivers. Then all the rivers joined together and became an angry ocean. The once-dry land was overwhelmed, and hills and homes were gone forever.

Noah and the animals watched through the
windows, safe and dry inside their ark.

For forty days and forty nights, it rained. The ark was pulled and pushed, up and down, to and fro on the rainwater ocean. Inside, the animals were frightened and Noah did his best to calm them. He trusted God and knew that all would be well in the end.

At long last, the rain stopped, just as God had said it would, and the ark lay still on the water. Then, strong winds began to blow. Little by little, the water level dropped and the tips of the mountains appeared. The ark came to rest on one of them—a mountain called Ararat. It seemed that the ark's journey was over.

Noah watched from a window, as land continued to appear. Then he sent a raven out into the world to see what it could find. An hour later, it came back tired and worn—and Noah knew there was nowhere for it to land.

A week later, Noah sent out a dove. After some hours, it returned with an olive twig in its beak—and Noah knew it had found at least one tree with branches above the water. It meant that Earth was drying out.

"Not long to wait now," he thought.

After one more week, Noah sent out the dove again. This time, the bird did not return—and Noah knew it had found a dry place to land.

"Now it is safe to leave the ark," he said to his family.

Noah flung open the doors, and all the animals filed out of the ark. They raced away in all directions, glad to stretch their legs and run free. The birds flew off to find twigs to build new nests, and the deer trotted off to search for fresh, green grass to eat. The giraffes walked and the lions ran, the monkeys scampered, and the kangaroos hopped. Soon, they would all find new homes and raise their families on the new, dry land.

After all the animals had left the ark, Noah and his family left, too. Noah wanted to thank God, so he built an altar of stones and bowed his head to pray.

"You saved me from the flood and brought me to dry land again," said Noah. "I will always be thankful."

God heard Noah's prayer and was pleased.

"Now is the time for a new beginning on Earth," He said. "I bless you and your family, and I wish you well. You must have lots of children, so the world will be filled with people again. All Earth's riches are yours—the animals and plants, the land, and the seas. They belong to you, and you must take care of them."

"Thank you, God," said Noah.

"One more thing," God continued. "I promise that I will never send another flood to destroy the world. Look up and you will see a sign."

Noah looked up at the sky. The gray storm clouds drifted away and bright rays of sunlight shone for the first time since before the flood. As Noah watched, God made a brilliant rainbow appear, which stretched from one end of Earth to the other.

Then, God spoke again.

"Whenever you see a rainbow in the sky, you will remember this day and my promise to you. Now, Noah, go and begin your new life."

Full of joy and thankfulness, Noah walked down the mountain to join his family and the new beautiful world.

Now, when we see a rainbow in the sky, we remember God's promise to Noah. It's also a promise from God to us and to our beautiful world.

The Tower of Babel

Time went by, and Noah's family began to fill the world, just as God had wanted. There were grandchildren, great-grandchildren, and great-great-grandchildren.

Some of the family traveled to a place called Babylonia. They learned how to make bricks and built homes for themselves. They thought they were very clever.

One day, someone suggested that the Babylonians should build the tallest tower in the whole world, so that everyone would know how clever they were. It would be named the Tower of Babel. They quickly set to work.

God watched as the people built the tower. He watched the walls grow higher and higher, and it made Him very sad. He knew the people were not thinking about Him—they were thinking only about their own importance. Soon, they would become as wicked as the people were before the great flood.

God knew the people had to be able to talk to each other in order to build the tower. If they spoke in different languages, they wouldn't understand one another, and the building would have to stop. So God made all His people speak in different languages and sent them to live in other countries around the world. The people couldn't work together, and the tall Tower of Babel remained unfinished forever.

Abraham and Sarah

One of Noah's descendants was a man named Abraham. He was a good person who believed in God.

One day, God told Abraham to leave his home. Abraham trusted God, so he and his wife Sarah did as God said.

Their journey to find a new home took several months. Then God spoke to Abraham again.

"Look about you," He said. "All the land you can see will be yours forever. You will have as many children as there are stars in the sky. You will be the father of a great nation."

"How can that be?" asked Abraham. "My wife and I are too old to have children."

"Trust me," said God. "You will have a son."

A few years later, three strangers came to Abraham's house and he welcomed them inside.

"We have wonderful news for you," said the strangers. "In nine months' time, Sarah will have a baby son."

Nine months later, Sarah gave birth to a baby boy, named Isaac.

"God also promised that my family will become a great nation," thought Abraham, "and I know He always keeps His promises."

Sure enough, that is exactly what happened.

Jacob and Esau

Abraham's son Isaac grew up and married a woman named Rebekah. After they had been married for a while, Rebekah had twin boys, Esau and Jacob. Esau was Isaac's favorite child, but Rebekah loved Jacob more.

The twins grew up to be very different—they didn't even look alike! Jacob had smooth skin, but Esau's skin was hairy.

As Isaac grew old, he went blind. He knew he would die soon and wanted to bless Esau as the new head of the family, since he was the older twin. But Rebekah wanted Jacob to receive Isaac's blessing, so she made a plan. While Esau was out, Rebekah dressed Jacob in Esau's clothes. She covered his arms with goatskin, to make them seem hairy like his brother's. Then she sent him to Isaac.

When Isaac touched his son's hairy arm, he believed that it was Esau's, but the voice sounded wrong.

"Are you really Esau?" Isaac asked his son.

"Yes, I am Esau," Jacob lied to his father.

So Isaac gave his blessing to Jacob instead of Esau.

Esau was very angry when he found out what Jacob had done. In fact, Jacob was afraid his brother might kill him, so he ran away to stay with relatives.

Jacob had lied, and he had cheated his brother, but God didn't leave him. He had plans for Jacob, so He forgave him and helped him. One night, God came to Jacob in a dream. Jacob saw a staircase reaching up to heaven, with angels moving up and down it.

"I am the God of Abraham and Isaac," God said, "and I will make this land your home. I will bless you, your children, and your children's children. I will watch over you wherever you go, and I will bring you back home."

"If You protect me and bring me safely back home as You have said," Jacob prayed, "then You will always be my God."

In time, Jacob married and traveled home to Canaan. He was afraid that Esau was still angry with him, so he prayed to God that he and his brother would be friends. God heard his prayer, and Esau welcomed Jacob back home with open arms.

Jacob had twelve sons and, in time, they grew into a great nation. Many years later, the family came to be known as the "Children of Israel" or "Hebrews." God had kept His promise.

Joseph and His Coat of Many Colors

Of Jacob's twelve sons, Joseph was his favorite. Joseph was kind and helpful, and his mother Rachel had been Jacob's most beloved wife. She had died, and Jacob missed her very much, but Joseph reminded him of her every day.

Jacob's ten eldest sons were too busy to spend much time with him, and his youngest son Benjamin was too young, but Joseph, the second youngest, loved sitting and talking with his father. They were good friends as well as being father and son.

Jacob enjoyed showing Joseph how much he was loved. He bought him a special coat, woven in bright, beautiful colors, to keep him warm while he and his older brothers tended the sheep on the hills.

"Thank you, Father," said Joseph, hugging Jacob. "I love it!"

Joseph's brothers felt jealous, because Joseph was their father's favorite. They had only plain, threadbare jackets, so when they saw Joseph's new coat, they disliked him even more.

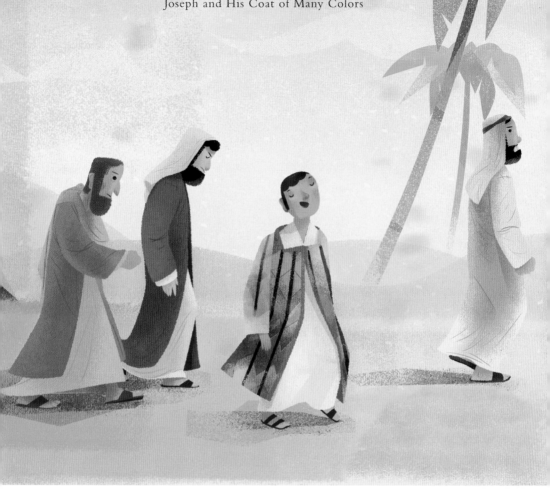

One day, the brothers were walking home from the hills to
help harvest the fields in Canaan, where they lived. Joseph's
brothers ignored him and muttered mean things about him.
But Joseph didn't notice that they were being unkind, because he
was thinking about a dream he had had the night before.

"I had a dream about the harvest last night," he said. "We each had a sheaf of golden corn standing in the field. Mine stood tall, while your smaller sheaves bowed down to it. I think it's a message from God. What do you think it means?"

His brothers were furious.

"Do you think you're better than us?" they asked.

Joseph felt terrible. He wanted his brothers to love him, but telling them about his dream had made them hate him even more.

A short time later, Joseph had another dream that he couldn't understand. He decided to tell his father and his brothers about it when they were all together at home. Perhaps his father would know what it meant.

"I had another dream last night," Joseph said one evening, trying to ignore the angry looks from his brothers. "This time, the Sun and Moon and eleven stars in the glittering night sky were bowing down to me. What could it mean?"

His brothers were enraged, and even his father frowned.

"Do you think that your brothers and I will come and bow down to you?" Jacob asked.

Joseph didn't dare to say any more, and Jacob didn't mention it again, but he didn't forget about Joseph's strange dream.

Over time, Joseph's brothers grew more and more jealous of Joseph. They left him out of everything and wanted to make him suffer for being their father's favorite.

One day, when the older brothers were out looking after the sheep and Benjamin was at home, Jacob sent Joseph to find out how they were doing. When the older brothers saw Joseph coming in his colorful coat, all their hateful feelings bubbled up.

"I've had enough of this dreamer," one brother snarled.

"If only we could get rid of him," said another.

"We could do what we liked to him out here," said a third. "We could say it was a wild animal. He might even die."

The others felt such hatred toward Joseph that hurting him suddenly didn't seem like such a bad thing to do. Only Reuben, Joseph's eldest brother, tried to stop them.

"Let's not kill him. Just throw him into a dry well," he said, thinking that he could rescue Joseph later when the others had calmed down.

The other brothers ripped Joseph's beautiful coat from his back and threw him into a dry well. But, while Reuben was tending to the sheep, they saw a group of travelers, called Ishmaelites, coming their way.

Another brother, Judah, had an idea. "We won't gain anything from killing Joseph," he said. "Let's sell him!"

So the greedy brothers sold Joseph for twenty pieces of silver. Shocked and hurt, Joseph was carried far away.

Joseph and His Coat of Many Colors

Reuben was horrified when he found out what his brothers had done. "How can we explain this to our father?" he cried.

"We'll make it sound like an accident," said Judah.

The brothers dipped Joseph's coat in animal blood, so it looked as if a wild beast had eaten him. Then, they took it home to Jacob. Believing that his dearest son was dead, Jacob's heart broke into pieces.

"I will go to my grave mourning for my son," he said.

Joseph was taken far away to Egypt. He was sold as a slave to a man named Potiphar. Potiphar was an important man who worked for Pharaoh, who was in charge of all Egypt.

"I am now a slave," Joseph said to himself. "It must be God's plan for me."

At first, Joseph's life in Egypt was not too bad. Joseph knew that God would want him to do his best. He worked hard and soon became an important servant. God blessed Potiphar's house, because Joseph was there.

His master Potiphar trusted him and everyone liked him—everyone except Potiphar's wife. Filled with wickedness and jealousy, she told Potiphar lies about Joseph to get him into trouble. Poor Joseph was thrown into prison.

But Joseph did not feel alone in prison, because God stayed with him. He made friends among the other prisoners, too.

One day, Joseph heard two other prisoners talking in worried voices. They were Pharaoh's butler and baker, and they had each had a strange dream on the same night.

"I understand a little about dreams," he said. "May I try to help?"

"I dreamed I saw a vine with three branches heavy with ripe grapes," the butler said. "I squeezed the juice from the grapes into Pharaoh's cup."

"That's simple," said Joseph. "In three days, Pharaoh will set you free."

Next, the baker told Joseph his dream.

"I had three baskets of bread for Pharaoh," he said. "But birds swooped out of the sky and ate them all."

"I'm sorry," said Joseph, his heart aching for the man. "In three days, Pharaoh will have you killed."

Everything that Joseph said came true.

Two years later, Pharaoh dreamed that seven fat cows came out of the River Nile. After them came seven thin and bony cows, which ate up the fat cows.

The same night, Pharaoh dreamed of seven healthy ears of corn. Another seven ears of corn sprouted, tiny and shriveled, and swallowed up the healthy corn.

"Who can tell me what these dreams mean?" cried Pharaoh.

Pharaoh's butler suddenly remembered the man in prison who

Pharaoh sent for Joseph and described his dreams to him.

"God is sending you a message," Joseph explained. "Seven years of good harvests are coming, followed by seven years of terrible famine."

Seeing that Joseph was a man of God, Pharaoh freed Joseph and put him in charge of saving Egypt. Joseph became rich and important. He made sure that enough grain was stored up from the good harvests to feed the Egyptian people through the hard years.

Just as Joseph had foreseen, seven years of plenty were followed by terrible famine. People outside of Egypt began to starve. In Canaan, Jacob and his sons were weak and hungry.

"Egypt has plenty of grain," Jacob told his sons. "Surely they can spare some for us?"

So the ten eldest sons set off for Egypt, leaving Benjamin at home.

Joseph was in charge of selling grain to people.

When the brothers reached Egypt, they bowed down before Joseph. Not one of them recognized him.

"It's just like my dream," Joseph thought. "At last I understand God's plan."

"We want to buy some grain," the brothers said.

Joseph hoped that his brothers had changed, and thought of a way to find out. "I think you're spies," he said.

"No, we are all brothers," they cried. "Once there were twelve of us, but one is dead. Our youngest brother is with our father Jacob, in Canaan."

"Bring your youngest brother to me, to prove that your story is true," Joseph said. "Otherwise, I will have you all killed."

He sent the brothers home with sacks of food. But he kept his brother Simeon in Egypt, to make sure that the others would return.

"This is God's punishment for the way we treated Joseph," the brothers whispered to each other.

Tears came to Joseph's eyes when he saw the fear on their faces.

At first, Jacob refused to let Benjamin go to Egypt. Since he had lost Joseph, Benjamin had become Jacob's favorite son, and he didn't want to lose him, even if it meant Simeon would have to stay in Egypt.

But, when they eventually ran out of food, he had to agree.

The brothers returned to Egypt with Benjamin. Joseph released Simeon and invited them all to eat at his house. Then he filled their sacks with food, refusing to accept their money. Secretly, Joseph asked a servant to hide a silver cup in Benjamin's sack of food.

Eventually, the brothers got up to leave.

"Stop!" Joseph yelled. "One of you has stolen my silver cup. Guards, search their sacks!"

When the cup was found in Benjamin's sack, the brothers dropped to their knees in front of Joseph.

"Please, imprison one of us instead," they begged. "Losing Benjamin would break our father's heart."

Joseph listened to them plead for Benjamin's life, and knew for certain that they had changed. Tears rolled down his cheeks as he kneeled down beside his brothers.

"Don't you recognize me?" he whispered.

When Joseph's brothers realized who he was, they couldn't speak for shock and shame. But Joseph smiled at them. He knew that this was all part of God's plan.

"I forgive you," he said.

Trembling, his brothers rose and hugged him. Then Joseph asked them to return to Canaan to tell Jacob the good news.

"Bring your families and all your animals back to Egypt," he said. "I will give you the best land here."

When Jacob heard that Joseph was alive, he could hardly believe it. It wasn't until he was standing in front of his beloved son that he knew it was true.

"Father!" cried Joseph, his heart bursting with joy.

They wrapped their arms around each other and wept happy tears. God had brought them back together at last.

Jacob settled comfortably in Egypt, in the region of Goshen, and lived to be a great age.

Moses

After Joseph died, life became very hard for the Israelites in Egypt. There was a new Pharaoh, who was afraid that there were too many of them and that they would turn against the Egyptians, so he made them into slaves. Then Pharaoh ordered that all their baby boys should be killed!

One mother, Jochebed, hid her baby in a basket beside the river—where Pharaoh's daughter found him. Pharaoh's daughter wanted to save the baby's life, so she took him to live with her in the palace. She named him Moses and asked Jochebed to be his nurse. She didn't know that Jochebed was Moses' real mother— it was God's plan that the boy should grow up with his mother beside him. As Moses grew up, his mother secretly told him that he was an Israelite.

One day, Moses attacked a cruel Egyptian master who was beating an Israelite slave. He knew he would be punished by Pharaoh for helping an Israelite, so he ran away to live as a shepherd in the desert.

Many years later, God spoke to Moses.

"I am the God of Abraham, Isaac, and Jacob," He said. "I have seen how My people are suffering, and I want you to go back to Egypt. Tell Pharaoh that he must free the Israelites and let them leave Egypt."

Moses was scared to go back to Egypt, but he could not refuse his God. So he went to Pharaoh and asked him to let the Israelites go. Pharaoh refused.

With that, God decided to punish Pharaoh by sending terrible disasters called plagues to destroy Egypt. The land was attacked by insects and frogs, the crops died, and the people became very sick. Only the Israelites were saved from these plagues.

But proud Pharaoh still would not free the Israelites. So God sent the angel of death to kill the eldest son of every Egyptian family. Pharaoh's son died, too. Only Israelite families were spared.

After this, Pharaoh agreed to let the Israelites go free. But then he changed his mind and sent his soldiers to capture them again! The only way they could escape was across the Red Sea. Moses stretched out his arms and God parted the waters, so that they could cross safely, into the desert on the other side. But when the soldiers tried to follow them, God made the water pour down on their heads and every one of them was killed.

The Israelites were free at last! God had kept His promise.

Moses and the Israelites

Thanks to God, the Israelites were free from Egypt, but they were still suffering, because there was no food in the desert.

"We would rather have died in Egypt than starve to death here," they moaned. God heard them, and made them a promise.

"I will give you meat every night and bread every day, except on the Sabbath—my day of rest," He said.

That night, a huge flock of birds appeared. They were easy to catch, so the Israelites had plenty of meat to eat.

The next morning, the ground was covered with white, bread-like flakes. They appeared every morning after that and were sweet to eat. The Israelites called them "manna."

Now, the Israelites had food to eat, but no water to drink. The hot sun beat down, and they became thirstier and thirstier.

Moses asked God for help.

"Find a rock at Mount Sinai," said God, "and hit it with your stick."

When Moses did as God had told him, water gushed out of the rock. Now, there was lots of cool, refreshing water for everyone to drink, and the people were happy.

Moses and the Israelites set up camp at the foot of Mount Sinai.

Then, one day, God spoke to them again.

"I have brought you here to be My chosen people," He said. "Will you obey Me?"

"We will," said the Israelites.

"Then I will give you ten special laws, called commandments," said God, "which show you how to serve Me and how to live together."

Two days later, thunder rumbled and lightning flashed at the top of the mountain.

Together, Moses and his brother Aaron climbed the mountain.
When they reached the top, God gave Moses the
Ten Commandments carved on two stone tablets.
These are God's ten laws:

1. Honor and serve Me alone,
   for I am the only God.
2. Do not make or worship
   any other gods.
3. Treat My name with respect.
4. Keep every Sabbath as a day
   of rest.
5. Respect your father and mother.
6. Do not kill another human being.
7. Husbands and wives must keep
   their love only for each other.
8. Do not steal.
9. Do not tell lies.
10. Do not be greedy about things
    that other people have.

God told Moses how the laws worked, and Moses explained
them to the people. He was God's special messenger, called
a "prophet."

"God loves you," Moses told the people, "and will look after
you as long as you honor Him and obey His laws."

The Israelites Conquer Jericho

The Israelites lived in the desert for forty years. Moses grew old and died, and God chose Joshua to be the new leader.

One day, God said to Joshua, "You must cross the River Jordan into the land I promised you and capture the city of Jericho."

The Israelites traveled to Jericho. The city walls were high and thick with strong gates, and there were soldiers on guard. It looked impossible for the Israelites to capture this city. But God told Joshua exactly what to do.

"Each day, for six days, you must march around the city. Seven priests must go first, blowing their trumpets. On the seventh day, march around the city seven times. Then, the priests must play one long note on their trumpets, and all the people must shout. The walls of Jericho will fall and the city will be yours!"

The Israelites did what God said. Down crashed the walls, and the Israelites captured the city!

This was the first of Joshua's great victories in Canaan. With him as their leader, the Israelites took over the Promised Land— the land that God had promised to Abraham many years before.

The First King of Israel

Many years later, God chose the prophet Samuel to lead the Israelites. Samuel was a fair leader. He loved God and he loved the honest way of life of his people. But the Israelites wanted a king, as other nations had.

Even though Samuel told them that a king might not treat them well, the people insisted. So God told Samuel, "I will give them what they want."

The young man God chose to be king of Israel was named Saul. He was a poor Israelite whose job was to look after his father's donkeys—he had no idea that he was God's chosen king. But Samuel reassured him and told him to trust in God.

In the beginning, Saul was a good ruler, but sadly that did not last. He soon became proud, and thought less about God and more about himself. He was so proud that, when he won battles against Israel's enemies, he thought it was because he was clever, not because God was helping him.

In the middle of one battle, Saul ordered that none of his soldiers should eat until they had won the fight. Anyone who ate would be killed, he said. But Saul's son Jonathan didn't hear the order. He was leading a group of soldiers on the battlefield, and none of them had eaten anything all day. He was hungry, so, when he found a honeycomb, he ate some of the sweet honey. The soldiers with him were shocked at what he had done.

"Didn't you hear the king's command?" they asked. "Anyone who eats before the battle is over must be put to death."

When proud Saul found out that Jonathan had disobeyed him, he would not go back on his word, even to save his own son's life! It was only when the Israelite people stood up to Saul that Jonathan's life was spared.

Even after this, Saul did not change his ways. He did exactly what he wanted, disobeyed God, and would not listen to Samuel. He won more victories—not for God, but to satisfy his own pride and greed.

At last, God decided to find a new king to replace Saul.

David and Goliath

God chose a young man named David to be the new king, but there were other things God needed him to do before he took the throne. God loved David, and was always with him.

David was a shepherd. He was a great shot with a slingshot, because he used it every day to protect his father's sheep from fierce lions and bears. He was clever in other ways, too. He was famous for playing the harp, and he was summoned to the palace to play for King Saul.

"Can you soothe the king with your playing?" one of Saul's servants asked David. "He is in a terrible mood."

"Of course," answered David, and began to play. Sure enough, when the king heard David's sweet music, he quickly became calmer and happier.

Far away, King Saul's battle with the Philistines was not going well. The Philistines had a fierce warrior named Goliath on their side—he was three meters tall, and much stronger than an ox! He was very proud, too.

"Send your greatest warrior to fight me!" Goliath sneered. "If he kills me, we Philistines will be your slaves. If I kill him, you will be ours."

Only David was brave enough to take up the challenge. He knew that God would protect him.

On the day of the fight, Saul offered David his own armor and sword, but David preferred to fight without it. He picked up his slingshot, put five smooth stones in a pouch on his belt, and set off to find Goliath.

Goliath laughed when he saw David. "The Israelites' greatest fighter is a boy with a slingshot!" he said.

But David stood his ground. "I come in the name of the God of Israel," he said. "I am not afraid!"

As Goliath moved closer to attack him, David pulled one of the small stones from his pouch, put it in his slingshot, took aim, and fired. The stone hit Goliath right between the eyes, making him lose his balance and fall to the ground.

He was dead.

When the Philistine army saw this, they ran away into the hills. The Israelites had won!

David and Goliath

Years later, after Saul died, David became the new king. His greatest wish was to conquer the city of Jerusalem, so he could keep the sacred box of God's laws there—a box containing the two stone tablets with the Ten Commandments written on them. After many years, he succeeded. He built a royal palace there and made Jerusalem God's city.

King Solomon

God loved King David and promised him that his sons would always be kings. So David told his son Solomon, "When I die, you must be a strong king, trust in God, and follow His commands. Then God will keep His promise." Solomon agreed to follow his father's advice.

In time, Solomon became king and, one night, he dreamt that God asked him, "What do you need from Me?"

Solomon replied, "I am very young to rule over so many people. Please give me wisdom to make right and true decisions."

This answer pleased God, and He gave Solomon more wisdom and understanding than anyone had ever had before.

Solomon was a good king in the beginning, and he made Israel rich and peaceful. But, over the years, he changed. He became greedy and proud, and—even worse—he did not stay faithful to God.

Solomon had to be punished. When he died, God split the kingdom of Israel in two. The northern part was ruled by a man named Jeroboam, who had once been one of Solomon's servants. The southern part, a much smaller part of the kingdom, was named Judah, and was ruled by Solomon's son, Rehoboam.

Daniel and the Lions

Over many, many years, God's people began to disobey Him. They forgot that the land they were living in was a gift from Him. So God allowed Nebuchadnezzar, the King of Babylon, to capture Jerusalem. Many Israelites died or ran away, and there was famine in the city.

Nebuchadnezzar took many prisoners from Jerusalem back to Babylon, including a group of young men from noble Israelite families. One of them was named Daniel.

Daniel was a good man who loved God, and did his best to obey Him. Even though Daniel was living in Babylon, he stayed true to God.

After some years, the Persians captured Babylon, and their leader, Darius, became king. Daniel could read and write Babylonian, and had grown very wise, so he became one of Darius's chief advisors. He served the king well—too well, perhaps, for the other advisors grew jealous and plotted against him.

Daniel prayed to God every day, and the advisors decided that this was how they would get their revenge on him. They persuaded King Darius to make a terrible new law: if a person asked any god or human being, other than the king, for anything during the next thirty days, he would be thrown into a pit of lions!

Daniel heard about the law, but kept on praying to God. His enemies were delighted—their plan had worked! They rushed to tell the king that Daniel had disobeyed him.

Darius was very sad, because he liked Daniel, but Daniel had broken the law. There was no way to save him. So, at sunset, Daniel was thrown into a pit full of hungry lions.

The king felt terrible that night. He could not rest, thinking about Daniel. As soon as dawn broke, he hurried to the lion pit. He called down into the pit, "Daniel, was your God able to save you from the lions?" He thought that Daniel must be dead, so he didn't expect an answer—but, to his amazement, he heard a voice!

"Your Majesty," said Daniel, "God knew that I was innocent and He has kept me safe. I have done you no wrong."

Daniel was freed at once, and the men who had accused him were thrown to the lions instead. Then, Darius made a new law: "Let everyone in my kingdom fear and respect the God of Daniel, for He is the one true, living God."

Daniel and the Lions

Jonah and the Whale

Jonah lived a simple life in a small village and kept to himself. He liked to sit in the sun outside his house and feed the birds. He didn't like to get involved in other people's problems.

But, one day, Jonah heard a voice that seemed to come from nowhere.

"Jonah, son of Amittai, you will be my prophet," it said.

Jonah jumped to his feet and looked around, but he could see no one.

Then, the voice spoke again, and Jonah knew that it was the voice of God.

"Go to the city of Nineveh and tell the people that they have been very wicked," God said. "Tell them that, if they don't change their ways, I will destroy the city."

Jonah shook with fear.

"Me?" he thought. "God wants me to leave here and go all the way to Nineveh? Who would listen to an unimportant Israelite like me?"

He didn't care about the Ninevites, their wickedness, or their city, and he thought they deserved to be punished by God. Why would God have chosen him? It must be a mistake. Jonah decided to ignore the voice. But God cannot be ignored.

"Jonah, hurry yourself," He said. "Get yourself to Nineveh!"

Jonah gathered some food and water for the journey, but he felt worried and annoyed. The same thought kept running through his mind: "I don't want to get involved in the Ninevites' problems. I just want to be left alone."

Jonah decided to run away to avoid doing God's work. So he left his home, but he did not set out for Nineveh. Instead, he headed for Joppa, a sea port, and got on a ship that was going to Tarshish.

"Maybe God won't notice that I am traveling in the wrong direction," Jonah thought. "By the time I get to Tarshish, it will be too late. I will be so far away from Nineveh that God will have to find Himself a new prophet!"

The sun beat down on Jonah's face and he started to relax. Perhaps he really could avoid God's plan for him. The ship left Joppa, and Jonah heaved a sigh of relief.

But God could read Jonah's thoughts, and He knew that His prophet was trying to escape. He made the wind blow stronger and stronger, until the ship was in the heart of a terrible storm.

The ship creaked and rocked as if it would tear apart. Terrified, the sailors threw the cargo into the sea to lighten the load, but the mighty waves just grew higher.

In his bunk, Jonah shivered, knowing that God had sent the storm because he had not done what God told him to do. Jonah got out of his bed and staggered up to the deck. Colossal waves were breaking right across the ship, and the sailors were clinging on for dear life. When Jonah saw how frightened they were, he felt very guilty.

"This is all my fault," he shouted above the roar of the ocean. "I have made God angry. Throw me overboard and save yourselves."

At first, the captain refused to throw his passenger overboard, but the sea became wilder. Hail lashed the decks, and bitter winds tore at the sailors. Desperate to save their lives, the sailors pushed Jonah into the cold sea.

"God, help me, please!" cried Jonah as he fell.

Water closed over Jonah's head, and filled his nose and mouth. He rose to the surface, coughing and spluttering. Although he was frightened, he could see that the sea was growing calmer and the wind dying down. The hail had stopped.

"Thank goodness," said Jonah. "Whatever happens to me, the ship and all the sailors are safe."

Suddenly, Jonah felt himself being sucked into darkness.
"I'm going to drown!" he thought.

Jonah and the Whale

He stretched out his arms as he was pulled down, and felt soft, warm walls all around him. In a panic, he kicked his legs and flailed his arms, but still he was pulled further down.

At last, Jonah landed on something soft and staggered to his feet.

"Where am I?" he whispered.

Looking around, he saw a vast, dim cavern that smelled of fish. A thin spear of light was shining from above, and when Jonah looked up he saw a hole high over his head.

Then he felt the cavern move, and he realized the truth in a flash of amazement: Jonah had been swallowed by a whale!

God had seen His prophet alone and helpless in the sea. He was pleased that Jonah had sacrificed himself to save the sailors, so He sent the whale to keep Jonah safe.

Kneeling down, Jonah spoke to God. "I am sorry for disobeying you," he said. "Please let me out of here!"

There was no reply. Jonah beat his hands against the side of the whale, but he could not escape.

Jonah lay inside the whale for three days and three nights. He was tired, wet, and cold, and he felt weak with hunger and thirst. Worst of all, he was gripped by fear. What if he were stuck inside the whale forever? What was God's plan for him?

At last, Jonah shut his eyes and prayed.

"God, I am ready," he whispered into the darkness. "I will gladly do what you asked."

Suddenly, everything started to shake, and light flooded the cavern. Jonah squeezed his eyes shut as he tumbled head over heels through the whale.

"What is happening?" he cried.

When Jonah opened his eyes, he was lying on soft, warm sand. The whale had thrown him up onto dry land. Then Jonah heard God's voice once again.

"Go to the city of Nineveh, Jonah," said God. "Do what I have asked of you."

"I will," Jonah promised.

He climbed to his feet and set off right away.

When he arrived in Nineveh, Jonah thought that no one would believe he was a prophet. But he kept his promise and preached in marketplaces. He spread God's message from slums to palaces, in temples, and in shacks.

"Turn to God and repent, or He will punish you," Jonah told the people.

To his surprise, people stopped to hear him speak. They believed what he said, and God's word spread. Even the King of Nineveh listened to Jonah's message. He changed his royal robes for clothes made of sackcloth, to show how sad he was.

"No one in Nineveh will eat or drink until we have shown God that we are sorry for all the things we have done wrong," said the king. "I hope that He will be able to forgive us."

God heard Nineveh's prayers and was pleased with Jonah.

"I will not destroy the city," He told Jonah. "They have obeyed me, so I will show mercy."

But, instead of feeling proud of having helped save the city, Jonah felt anger raging inside him. Why hadn't the Ninevites been punished?

"The Ninevites don't deserve to be forgiven!" he cried.

"Is it right for you to be angry?" asked God.

Jonah did not reply. He stormed out of the city—but soon the scorching midday sun was burning down on his head.

Jonah staggered to the side of the road and dropped to the ground under a bare tree. He was exhausted and furious, and there was no shelter from the sun.

"I wish I had never come here," he fumed. "I didn't ask to get involved."

As Jonah sat there in a rage, God made fresh, green leaves unfurl from the bare branches of the tree. The tree grew larger and curved itself over Jonah, until he was lying in its shade. As his body cooled down, his temper cooled, too.

"Thank you, God," he murmured as he drifted off to sleep.

At sunrise, God sent a worm to eat Jonah's tree. Its leaves shriveled up and fell from the branches. Jonah awoke to find the sun blazing down on him again.

"Why did you kill the tree, God?" Jonah raged. "It was a good tree and provided me with shelter."

"You are angry because the tree did not deserve to die," God said. "How would I have felt if I'd had to let Nineveh burn? If the tree deserves a second chance, surely my people deserve a second chance, too? And what about you, and the whale who saved you?"

Jonah bowed his head in shame. Now, he could see what God was trying to show him.

"I'm sorry," he whispered.

God had saved the people of Nineveh, just as He had sent the whale to save Jonah, because God loves all His people.

The New Testament

The Christmas Story

Long ago, in a place called Nazareth, there lived a young woman named Mary. She was engaged to be married to Joseph, a carpenter, and loved to daydream about their future life together.

One day, as she swept her yard, Mary noticed a stranger smiling at her. She didn't know who he was, and she was frightened.

"My name is Gabriel," the stranger said. "I have brought you a message from God."

Mary was too amazed to speak.

"Don't be afraid," said Gabriel. "God has chosen you to do something special for Him. Soon, you will have a baby. He will be God's own son and he will be king. You are to call him Jesus."

Mary trusted God, so she agreed to do what He asked of her.
But Joseph felt upset, because he knew he wasn't the father of
the baby.

"I love Mary, but I don't know if I should still marry her,"
he thought. So he prayed to God for help.

God heard his prayers and, that night, He sent an angel to visit
Joseph in a dream.

The angel was gentle and kind.

"Do not worry, Joseph," he said. "You should marry Mary and
love her as your wife. She is the most special of women, chosen by
God to be the mother of His son. The baby will be named Jesus,
which means 'savior,' because he will save his people."

When Joseph woke up, he decided to marry Mary right away.

"I trust in God," he said to himself.

So Mary and Joseph were married, and they waited patiently
for the baby to arrive.

Soon after the wedding, Emperor Augustus, who ruled over the land where Mary and Joseph lived, decided to make a list of all the people in his empire to make sure they paid their taxes. He sent out orders through his messengers to every town and city in the land.

"Everyone must travel back to the place they were born to be counted," said the messengers.

Joseph had been born in Bethlehem, far away from Nazareth.

"My wife can't travel now—she's going to have a baby soon," Joseph said to the messenger. "She should stay home in comfort, not travel far away. Can we go to Bethlehem another time?"

The messenger shook his head.

"No," he said sternly. "This is the Emperor's order. You must go now."

The journey to Bethlehem took many days. The roads were bone-dry and dusty, and the sun beat down. Often, Mary had to stop and rest.

At last, late one night, they arrived in Bethlehem. Joseph looked at Mary and saw how tired she was.

"We'll find a place to stay for the night," he reassured her. But Bethlehem was packed with people who had followed the Emperor's orders, and every inn they tried was full.

They reached the very last inn in town, but the innkeeper said,
"There is no room. You'll have to try somewhere else."

"What can we do?" pleaded Mary. "My baby is coming soon."

The innkeeper was a kind man and saw how tired Mary was.
"Come with me," he said. "I have a place that might do."

NO ROOM

The innkeeper led them to a barn behind the inn.

"I know it's not much," said the innkeeper, "but it's warm and dry."

Mary and Joseph looked inside. The barn was filled with animals and the floor was covered with fresh hay.

"My baby will be safe here," said Mary. "Thank you for your kindness."

Later that night, Mary gave birth to a little boy, the son of God, just as the angel had said. Joseph lined the manger with fresh hay to make a soft bed. Mary wrapped the baby in a blanket and laid him down there gently.

"We will love you and care for you, little one, and we will call you Jesus," whispered Mary.

High on a hillside nearby, some shepherds were looking after their sheep. The night was dark and still, and the sheep were dozing peacefully.

Suddenly, there was a dazzling brightness in the sky and an angel appeared.

"What's happening?" cried the shepherds, huddling together in fear.

"Do not be afraid," said the angel. "I have the most wonderful news for you and for all the people on Earth. The son of God has been born in Bethlehem. He is the king who will save humankind, just as God promised."

More angels appeared and sang, "Glory to God, and peace to everyone on Earth!"

Then, suddenly, the angels were gone. The shepherds looked at each other in wonder.

"Can it be true?" said one shepherd to another.

"Without a doubt," the second shepherd replied. "We must go to Bethlehem and see the baby at once."

The shepherds ran down from the hillside and through the dark streets of Bethlehem. They ran and ran, until at last they heard a baby's cry and found the barn where Jesus was sleeping.

"We have come to see the new king," they told Joseph excitedly. "God sent an angel to tell us about him."

"You are all welcome," said Joseph.

NO ROOM

NO ROOM

So the shepherds went inside and saw Mary with the tiny baby in the manger.

"Wonderful!" said the first shepherd.

"Our savior!" said the second, as they kneeled to gaze at him.

"We are poor. We have no gift for him," they said to Mary. "All we have to give him is our love."

"That is the very best gift in the world," said Mary.

Soon, it was time for the shepherds to return to their sheep. They were so excited that they told everyone they met about the new king.

That same night, a new star appeared in the sky. In a far-off land, three wise men looked up and saw it. They knew it meant that something very special had happened.

"The star must be a sign from God. It is shining because a new king has been born, just as He promised years ago," said the first. "We must go at once and worship him."

"Perhaps the star will lead us to the baby," said the second.

"Let's take him the most special gifts," said the third. "Gifts fit for a king."

Without delay, the wise men packed their bags, climbed on their camels, and rode off toward the city of Jerusalem. They were sure they would find the new king there, at the palace.

"Where else would a king be, but in the finest of palaces?" they said to each other.

The wise men traveled across many deserts for many nights, until they finally arrived at Jerusalem. They went to the palace and asked the guards to take them to the ruler, King Herod.

"Where is the new king?" they asked him. "We have traveled far, following the new star that appeared on the night of his birth."

King Herod was shocked. He was the only king in this land, and that was how he wanted it to stay.

"Who is this new king they speak of?" he whispered to his advisor.

"A prophet once said that, one day, a new king would be born in Bethlehem," said the advisor.

"This must not be," Herod thought to himself.

"I want to worship him, too," Herod lied to the wise men. "Go to Bethlehem, then come back and tell me where he is."

Herod didn't tell them, but he planned to stop the baby from taking his throne.

The wise men set off again into the night, and traveled to Bethlehem, where the star led them to Mary, Joseph, and Jesus.

"We have come to see the new king," they said to Joseph.

"You are most welcome," said Joseph.

The wise men stepped inside and saw Mary with her tiny baby, the son of God. Quietly, the wise men kneeled down to give the baby their gifts.

"Here is precious gold," said the first.

"I have brought sweet-smelling frankincense," said the second.

"And this is myrrh, a healing oil," said the third.

"You will be a great king, a teacher, a leader, and you will save all the people of the Earth," they said to Jesus together.

Then, the wise men said goodbye and found a place to rest before starting their journey home.

While the wise men slept, God visited each of them in a dream. He warned them not to return to Herod. So, in the morning, the wise men went straight home and did not return to Jerusalem.

When King Herod learned that the wise men had disobeyed him, he was furious.

"I am the only king!" he roared. "I will not let a baby take my throne!"

Jesus was not safe in Bethlehem now, so God sent an angel to visit Joseph while he slept.

"You must wake up!" the angel said to Joseph. "Escape to Egypt, where you will be safe. Stay there until I tell you to come back."

Joseph woke Mary, and they quickly loaded their belongings onto a donkey. Then, with Mary carrying Jesus tightly in her arms, they set off into the night.

Jesus was safe in Egypt, and he lived there with Mary and Joseph peacefully for some years. His parents missed their home in Nazareth, but, while King Herod was alive, they knew they could never return.

Then, one day, Herod died and Joseph had a dream. An angel appeared to him and said, "Joseph, it is safe for you to return home."

Joseph and Mary were overjoyed. They packed up all their belongings and set off once more, with Jesus by their side.

When they arrived, they were glad to be back in their home town at last.

Joseph held Jesus as he stood in the doorway of their little house.

"This is Nazareth, the town where you will grow up," he said with a smile. "Welcome home, Jesus!"

Jesus Visits the Temple

When Jesus was twelve years old, Mary and Joseph took him to Jerusalem for the Festival of Passover. The celebrations lasted a whole week.

After the festival, everyone began the long journey back to Nazareth. Mary and Joseph were walking with many other people, and at the end of the day they realized that they hadn't seen Jesus for a long while. They searched for him, but he was nowhere to be seen, so they hurried back to Jerusalem, hoping to find him there.

It was three days before they found Jesus—he was in the temple, calmly listening to the men who taught God's laws, and asking questions. Everyone was amazed at how much of the teaching he understood!

"We have been searching everywhere for you," said Mary. "We have been so worried. How could you do this to us?"

Jesus was surprised. "I'm sorry you were worried," he said, "but I felt so at home here in my Father's house, I stayed here."

Mary and Joseph were pleased that he was safe, and they set off again for Nazareth, with Jesus walking beside them all the way.

Jesus Is Baptized

Just before Jesus was born, Mary's cousin Elizabeth had given birth to a son named John. When John grew up, God spoke to him and said, "You will be My messenger. You will preach My word to the people."

John did so, and people traveled from far and wide to hear him speak.

"God's king is coming soon," he told them. "Tell God that you are sorry for your sins. Change your ways, then He will forgive you."

Many people were sorry for their sins, so John led them to the River Jordan and dipped their heads under the water. This was a sign that their sins had been washed away. It was called "baptism."

"Are you God's promised king?" people asked him.

"No," said John. "I am only a messenger. Someone much greater than me is coming soon."

One day, Jesus came to John and said, "Will you baptize me, too?"

They had never met before, but John knew at once that this was Jesus, God's promised king.

"*You* should baptize *me*, Lord," he said, falling to his knees.

"No, John," said Jesus. "I want the people to see me baptized and to know that it is important."

So John did as Jesus asked, and God was pleased.

Simon
(renamed Peter)

Andrew
(brother of Simon)

James
(son of Zebedee)

John
(brother of James)

Philip

Bartholomew

Thomas

Matthew

James
(son of Alphaeus)

Thaddeus or Judas
(son of James)

Simon
the Zealot

Judas Iscariot

Jesus and His Disciples

One morning, as Jesus walked beside Lake Galilee, he saw two fishermen pulling their fishing boats up onto the beach nearby.

"Will you take me out onto the lake?" Jesus asked them.

One of them, whose name was Simon, agreed, and Jesus began to teach from the boat. People stopped to listen along the shore.

When Jesus had finished teaching, he told Simon to row further out and drop the fishing nets there.

"We didn't catch any fish there all last night," said Simon, "but we will do as you ask."

So Simon and his brother Andrew rowed out into the middle of the lake and dropped their nets. Instantly, the nets were teeming with wriggling fish. There were so many that Simon thought the boat might sink.

"James! John!" he called to two more fishermen nearby. "We need help!"

All four fishermen were amazed to see all the fish. They knew that they were watching something very special.

Then, Jesus said to them, "Come and follow me. From now on, you will work with people, not fish."

After this, Jesus called other people to follow him, too. Altogether, he chose twelve men to be his closest companions and share his work. They were called his "disciples."

Jesus Feeds 5,000 People

As time passed, more and more people came to listen to Jesus. He would speak to the crowds for hours at a time.

One day, Jesus was teaching by Lake Galilee. The day wore on and, by sunset, 5,000 people or more were gathered around him. It had been a long day, and they were all very hungry.

"Please send the people away," the disciples begged Jesus. "Tell them to walk to the farms and villages to find food."

But Jesus replied, "Why don't you give them food?"

Jesus's disciple Andrew stepped forward.

"This boy is offering five loaves and two fish, but that won't be enough to feed this crowd!" he said.

Jesus took the loaves and fish, and thanked God for them. Then, he gave the food to the disciples, who broke it up and handed it out to the people. Everyone ate as much as they wanted and, when they had finished, the disciples gathered up twelve full baskets of leftover food. It was a miracle!

Jesus Walks on Water

After this wonderful meal, Jesus told his disciples to climb into their boat and go to the other side of the lake, while he said goodbye to the crowd. Then, he went into the hills to pray.

Later that night, as the wind got stronger, the disciples in the boat saw someone walking toward them over the water.

They were terrified. "It's a ghost!" they cried.

But Jesus called to them, "Don't be afraid. It is me."

Peter said, "If this is really you, Lord, tell me to come to you over the water."

"Come, Peter," said Jesus.

So Peter got out of the boat and walked toward Jesus over the water. He watched Jesus at first, but when he noticed the waves and the wind, he became afraid and began to sink. "Save me, Lord!" he cried.

Immediately, Jesus reached out his hand to Peter and caught hold of him. "How little faith you have," he said. "Why did you doubt me? Let's get back to the boat."

As they did so, the wind stopped and the water was calm. Everyone in the boat was amazed and said to each other, "This must truly be God's son."

The Easter Story

It was a very exciting day in Jerusalem. Riding on a humble donkey, Jesus had arrived in the city for the Festival of Passover. Cheers rang out from the crowd and palm leaves waved in the air. Everyone had come to see their king entering the city.

"God bless the king who comes in the name of the Lord!"
they shouted.

Many people laid palm leaves down for the donkey to walk
upon. Everyone wanted to show their love and respect.

Jesus went straight to the city's temple, where he got a terrible shock. In the temple's courtyard, people were buying goods, changing money, and selling animals. It was noisy and smelly. The air was filled with the shouts of sellers and the cries of animals. Jesus felt anger rise up inside him.

"The house of God is a house of prayer," he roared. "But you have turned it into a den of greed!"

He turned over the tables of goods, and coins rained down to the ground. The sellers scurried away, making room for people to pray. Jesus's supporters cheered, but the chief priests were furious.

"He wants to destroy our power over the people," they snarled.

The priests controlled people by making them afraid, but people listened to Jesus because he talked about love.

"If only we could get rid of him," the priests muttered.

Six days before the Festival of Passover, Jesus and his disciples went to stay with some friends. They were served a special meal and, while they relaxed around the table, a woman opened a jar of expensive perfumed oil. She kneeled down and rubbed the oil onto Jesus's feet.

"You could have sold that and given the money to the poor," snapped Judas, one of Jesus's disciples.

"Leave her alone," said Jesus. "She is being kind."

But Judas felt angry with Jesus, and his anger allowed evil to creep into his heart. He knew that the chief priests didn't like Jesus, and he decided to help them get rid of him. Two days before Passover, he met with them and agreed to lead them to Jesus when Jesus was alone.

"I will kiss Jesus to show the guards who to arrest," he told the priests.

In return, the priests promised to pay Judas thirty pieces of silver.

Jesus knew that the priests were plotting against him. He also knew that it was all part of God's plan, and that he would leave the world soon to join his Father in heaven. But he still felt sad when he thought about what was going to happen.

The evening before Passover, Jesus took some water and kneeled in front of each of the twelve disciples in turn. He gently washed their feet and dried them on a towel.

"Lord, you should not wash our feet," said the disciples. "You are too important."

"No one is more important than anyone else," Jesus said. "Even though I am your teacher, we are all equal, because we are all God's children."

On the day of Passover, Jesus and his disciples sat down to eat a special meal together.

"Soon, one of you will betray me," Jesus told them. The disciples were shocked—all except Judas.

"Who is it?" they asked. They didn't notice Judas turning pale.

But Jesus would not speak Judas's name. He blessed the bread by saying a prayer, then broke it into pieces and handed it to his disciples.

"Like this bread, my body will be broken," he said. "Please eat it."

He blessed the wine and passed around the cup, so they could all drink from it, to show they were part of God's family.

"This wine is like my blood, which will be spilled for many people," he said. "Please drink it."

As they ate and drank, Jesus watched his disciples with sadness in his heart.

"Eat and drink to remember me," he said. "We won't have another meal together until we are in God's kingdom."

There was a quiet garden called Gethsemane, where Jesus liked to pray. After the meal, he took Peter, James, and John there to pray with him. While they rested, Jesus fell to his knees to pray. He knew that the priests were coming for him, and he felt afraid.

"Father, I know what needs to happen, but it's going to be very hard," he said. "Please help me."

Jesus spoke to God for a long time and his disciples fell asleep.

Soon, Judas entered the garden. Judas was followed by men armed with swords and fiery torches.

"Rise!" Jesus called. "Here comes the traitor."

Peter, James, and John rose quickly, but it was too late. Judas walked up to Jesus and kissed his cheek. It was his signal to the guards that this was the man to arrest. The guards grabbed Jesus by the arms and held him tightly. Peter wanted to fight, but Jesus stopped him.

"My Father in heaven will protect me," he said.

The chief priests took Jesus to Pontius Pilate, the Roman governor. The Romans were in charge of Jerusalem, so it was Pilate's job to decide what would happen to prisoners.

Pilate questioned Jesus, trying to find out if Jesus was an enemy of Rome. He knew that the chief priests wanted Jesus dead, but he believed Jesus was harmless.

Early the next morning, a large crowd had gathered.

"Do you want me to release the King of the Jews?" Pilate asked them.

The chief priests had already talked to the crowd and told them lies about Jesus.

"No!" the people shouted. "Crucify him!"

"Why?" Pilate asked. "What crime has he committed?"

But the crowd just kept shouting, "Crucify him!"

Pilate was a weak man and he wanted to please the people. So he had Jesus beaten and then handed him over to be crucified.

The soldiers dressed Jesus in a purple robe to make fun of him. Purple was the color that kings wore, and they thought he had been pretending to be a king. They wanted to mock him and laugh at him. They even twisted together some thorns to make a crown.

"Hail, King of the Jews!" they shouted, laughing at him.

Jesus was forced to carry a heavy, wooden cross through the crowded city streets. All the way, people jeered and shouted at him. It was very different from the way he had arrived in Jerusalem.

At nine o'clock in the morning, the soldiers nailed Jesus to the cross.

"Father, forgive them," Jesus whispered. "They don't understand what they are doing."

The minutes crept by like hours and Jesus was in great pain. It became harder and harder for him to breathe. A crowd gathered, shouting nasty things at Jesus and making fun of him.

"If you were really the son of God, you would save yourself," they jeered. "Come down from the cross!"

Jesus did not reply. He felt as if each breath was tearing at his body. The sun shrank away, and the sky became dark and stormy, but the crowd and the priests kept shouting their cruel words.

Finally, at three o'clock, with a loud cry, the son of God took his last breath.

Later that day, a Roman named Joseph took down Jesus's body, wrapped it in linen, and placed it in a tomb. Then, he rolled a large, heavy stone over the entrance.

Early the next morning, Mary Magdalene, one of Jesus's friends, came to visit the tomb. To her amazement, she found that the large stone had been rolled away.

Mary stepped into the dark tomb and saw that Jesus's body was gone. All that was left were the strips of linen in which he had been wrapped.

"He is not here," said a voice.

Mary turned and saw a man dressed all in white. He was an angel, but she did not know that. She gasped in fear.

"Do not be afraid," the man said. "Jesus has risen! Go, tell his disciples."

Trembling with shock and overcome with happiness, Mary fled from the tomb, and ran to find Peter and John.

At first, Peter and John did not believe Mary's story. They followed her to the tomb and ran inside.

"Someone has stolen the body!" they cried. "Who could have done such a thing?"

They went to tell the other disciples what had happened, but Mary stayed behind.

"What shall I do?" she cried, tears running down her face.

She was afraid to be there alone, but she did not want to go home, either.

"Mary," said a familiar voice.

She knew Jesus's voice at once. But how could it be him? A man stepped forward.

"Master!" Mary cried, falling to her knees before him.

"Tell the disciples what you have seen," said Jesus. "I will soon be with my Father in heaven."

Mary ran back to find the disciples.

"I have seen my Lord with my own eyes," she cried. "He has risen from the grave!"

Over the next forty days, Jesus appeared many times to his disciples. On the Mount of Olives, near Jerusalem, he spoke to them one last time.

"It is time for me to return to my Father in heaven," he said. "Everything has happened just as He said it would. But I will always be with you."

The sun burst out from behind a bank of clouds. As golden beams of light dazzled them, the disciples watched Jesus rise up to heaven. Then, two angels appeared, dressed in shimmering white.

"Jesus will come back to you," they promised.

The disciples shared smiles of love and happiness. They knew that, until Jesus returned, they would keep his words alive. They would spread his message of love throughout the world.

Prayers

My World Is Wonderful

All things bright and beautiful,
All creatures, great and small,
All things wise and wonderful,
The Lord God made them all.

Each little flower that opens,
Each little bird that sings,
He made their glowing colors,
He made their tiny wings.

The tall trees in the greenwood,
The meadows where we play,
The rushes by the water
We gather every day—

He gave us eyes to see them,
And lips that we might tell
How great is God Almighty,
Who has made all things well.

CECIL FRANCES ALEXANDER (1818–1895)

Thank You, God, for showing me
The perfect beauty of a tree.
I didn't know a tree could be
Remarkable, like You and me.

Dear God,
Bless our nets as we cast and trawl;
The ocean is deep and our ship is small.

207

For flowers that bloom about our feet,
Father, we thank Thee.
For tender grass so fresh, so sweet,
Father, we thank Thee.
For the bird and hum of bee,
For all things fair we hear or see,
Father in heaven, we thank Thee.

RALPH WALDO EMERSON (1803–1882)

For air and sunshine, pure and sweet,
We thank our heavenly Father.
For grass that grows beneath our feet,
We thank our heavenly Father.
For lovely flowers and blossoms gay,
For trees and woods in bright array,
For birds that sing in joyful lay,
We thank our heavenly Father.

Tomorrow is a special day—
My family and I are going away!
We're going where there's sand and sea,
And ball games we can play with glee;
Where donkeys give rides on the beach,
And seagulls fly just out of reach;
Where Mom's skirt billows in the breeze,
And Dad gets wet up to his knees!
Thank You, God, for such good things,
For rocks and boats and rubber rings,
For sand and shells and sky and sun,
For the simple joy of having fun.

For this new morning and its light,
For rest and shelter of the night,
For health and food, for love and friends,
For every gift Your goodness sends,
We thank You, gracious Lord.

God made the world so broad and grand,
Filled with blessings from His hand.
He made the sky so high and blue,
And made the little children, too.

Dear God,
Thank You for the sun so bright,
Which fills the world with dazzling light.
And thank You for the muffled sound
When snow lies thickly on the ground.

A special thanks for gentle rain,
Which helps the grass grow green again.
But please, God, send the wind, I pray,
So I can fly my kite today.

The year's at the spring;
The day's at the morn;
Morning's at seven;
The hill-side's dew-pearled;
The lark's on the wing;
The snail's on the thorn;
God's in His heaven—
All's right with the world!

ROBERT BROWNING (1812–1889)

For all the rich autumnal glories spread—
The flaming pageant of the ripening woods,
The fiery gorse, the heather-purpled hills;
The rustling leaves that fly before the wind
And lie below the hedgerows whispering;
For meadows silver-white with hoary dew;
The first crisp breath of wonder in the air,
We thank You, Lord.

O, thought I!
What a beautiful thing
God has made winter to be
By stripping trees
And letting us see
Their shape and forms.
What a freedom does it seem
To give them to the storms.

DOROTHY WORDSWORTH (1771–1855)

Joy to the world!
The Lord is come;
Let Earth receive her King;
Let every heart
Prepare Him room,
And heav'n and nature sing,
And heav'n and nature sing,
And heav'n, and heav'n
And nature sing.

Joy to the world!
The Savior reigns;
Let men their songs employ,
While fields and floods,
Rocks, hills and plains
Repeat the sounding joy,
Repeat the sounding joy,
Repeat, repeat
The sounding joy.

ISAAC WATTS (1674–1748)

Praise the Lord! Ye heavens adore Him,
Praise Him, angels in the height!
Sun and Moon, rejoice before Him,
Praise Him, all ye stars and light.

JOHN KEMPTHORNE (1775–1838)

All things praise Thee, Lord most high!
Heaven and Earth and sea and sky!
Time and space are praising Thee!
All things praise Thee; Lord, may we!

GEORGE WILLIAM CONDER (1821–1874)

God bless the field and bless the furrow,
Stream and branch and rabbit burrow.
Bless the minnow, bless the whale,
Bless the rainbow and the hail,
Bless the nest and bless the leaf,
Bless the righteous and the thief,
Bless the wing and bless the fin,
Bless the air I travel in,
Bless the mill and bless the mouse,
Bless the miller's bricken house,
Bless the earth and bless the sea,
God bless you and God bless me.

Josie is my best friend;
She's never rude or cross.

Jamie is the tallest;
He thinks he is the boss.

Jason wears a white shirt
And gets his math all right.

Alice is the sweetest;
Her curls are small and tight.

All my friends are special;
They mean a lot to me.
And Jesus is my friend as well,
Because he cares for me.

Dear God,
I love to be on the beach
Where the sand meets the sea.
It reminds me what a wonderful world
You've made.

I can look far out,
Where the sea meets the sky,
And know that there's a wonderful world out there.
Perhaps, one day,
I'll go traveling and see the world.

Thank You for flowers;
Thank You for trees;
Thank You for grasses
That toss in the breeze.

Thank You for vegetables;
Thank You for spice;
Thank You for everything
That makes food taste nice.

Thank You, dear Father,
For all things that grow,
In sunshine and rain,
And the glowing rainbow.

I love to see the raindrops
Splashing on the sidewalks;
I love to see the sunlight
Twinkling in the rain;
I love to see the wind-gusts
Drying up the raindrops;
I love to feel the sunshine
Coming out again.

Thank You for the thunderstorm,
Thank You for the wind and rain,
And thank You for the sunshine
Coming out again.

Wide as the world,
(spread arms wide)

Deep as the sea,
(point down deep)

High as the sky,
(point up high)

Is Your love for me.
(hug yourself)

God bless our school.
Help our teachers.
Strengthen the principal.
And bless all the children.
Amen

I have
quiet friends,
noisy friends,
funny ones and sad,
many friends,
few friends,
sensible and mad,
good friends,
naughty friends,
tall friends and short;
thank You, God,
for giving me
friends of every sort.

When I travel in a bus,
I see the streets and houses.
When I go in a train,
I see the fields and hills.
When I fly in an airplane,
I can see the whole country.

If I could go up in a rocket,
I would see the whole world.
Thank You, God, for travel.
It shows me what a great world
You have made.

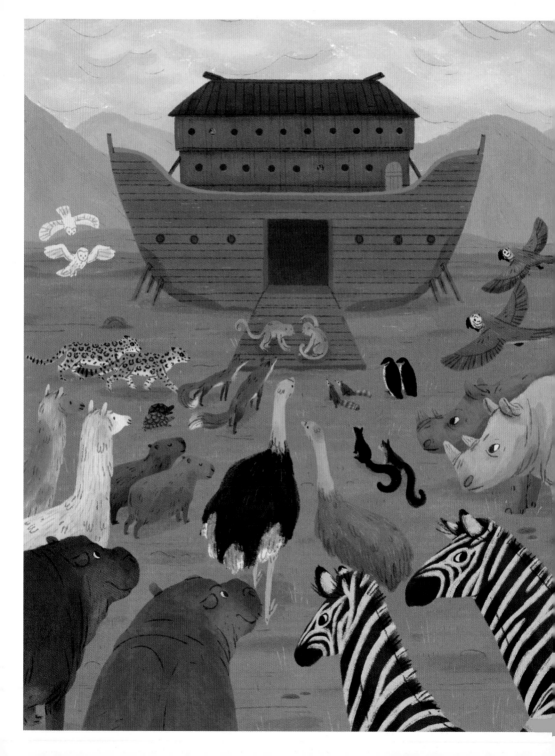

God Bless the Animals

Jesus, our brother, strong and good,
Was humbly laid in a manger of wood,
And the friendly beasts around Him stood,
Jesus, our brother, strong and good.

"I," said the donkey, shaggy and brown,
"I carried His mother uphill and down;
I carried her safely to Bethlehem town,
I," said the donkey, shaggy and brown.

"I," said the cow, all white and red,
"I gave Him my manger for His bed;
I gave Him my hay to pillow His head,
I," said the cow, all white and red.

"I," said the sheep with the curly horn,
"I gave Him my wool for His blanket warm;
He wore my coat on Christmas morn,
I," said the sheep with the curly horn.

"I," said the dove, from the rafters high,
"Cooed Him to sleep, my mate and I;
We cooed Him to sleep, my mate and I,
I," said the dove, from the rafters high.

And every beast, by some good spell,
In the stable dark was glad to tell
Of the gift he gave Immanuel,
The gift he gave Immanuel.

TWELFTH-CENTURY CAROL

Thank You, God, for giving us
The hippo and rhinoceros;
For crazy monkeys, brash and loud;
Giraffes with heads stuck in the clouds.
Thanks for parrots, bold and bright,
And zebras smart in black and white;
For elephants with giant feet,
And anteaters so trim and neat.
I wouldn't want the world to be
Empty except for You and me.

God Bless the Animals

241

The little cares that fretted me,
I lost them yesterday,
Among the fields above the sea,
Among the winds at play,
Among the lowing herds,
The rustling of the trees,
Among the singing of the birds,
The humming of the bees.

The foolish fears of what might pass,
I cast them away,
Among the clover-scented grass,
Among the new-mown hay,
Among the hushing of the corn,
Where the drowsy poppies nod,
Where ill thoughts die and good are born—
Out in the fields with God.

LOUISE IMOGEN GUINEY (1861–1920)

Little lamb, who made thee?
Dost thou know who made thee?
Gave thee life and bade thee feed
By the stream and over the mead;
Gave thee clothing of delight,
Softest clothing, woolly, bright;
Gave thee such a tender voice
Making all the vales rejoice?

Little lamb, who made thee?
Dost thou know who made thee?

Little lamb, I'll tell thee;
Little lamb, I'll tell thee;
He is called by thy name,
For He calls himself a Lamb;
He is meek and He is mild,
He became a little child.
I a child and thou a lamb,
We are called by His name,

Little lamb, God bless thee!
Little lamb, God bless thee!

WILLIAM BLAKE (1757–1827)

Hurt no living thing:
Ladybird, nor butterfly,
Nor moth with dusty wing,
Nor cricket chirping cheerily,
Nor grasshopper so light of leap,
Nor dancing gnat, nor beetle fat,
Nor harmless worms that creep.

CHRISTINA ROSSETTI (1830–1894)

He prayeth best, who loveth best
All things both great and small;
For the dear God who loveth us,
He made and loveth all.

Samuel Taylor Coleridge (1772–1834)

Dear Father,
Hear and bless
Thy beasts and singing birds,
And guard with tenderness
Small things that have no words.

Beetles are funny;
ants are, too;
flies have fantastic wings.
Sometimes, I like them,
so my prayer is,
"Thank You, God, for the smallest things."

Spiders are scary;
mice are, too;
moths have fluttery wings.
Sometimes, I hate them,
so I say, "Help me
not to be scared of the smallest things!"

When dogs bark and hamsters squeak,
Are they really trying to speak?
When hens and roosters cluck and crow,
Are they really in the know?
Dear God, do animals talk to You
And tell You what they'd like to do?
For, if they can't, I'd like to say,
Please watch over them today.

Loving Shepherd of Thy sheep,
Keep Thy lambs, in safety keep;
Nothing can Thy power withstand;
None that can pluck them from Thy hand.

JANE ELIZA LEESON (1807–1882)

To all the humble beasts there be,
To all the birds on land and sea,
Great Spirit, sweet protection give
That free and happy they may live!

God Bless the Animals

253

God bless the animals
Great and small,
And help us learn
To love them all.

Please listen to this special prayer,
And if I start to cry
It's because my budgie's ill
And I think he's going to die.
Nothing lives forever,
That is something I know.
But even though I know it,
I wish it wasn't so.

Please, God,
You know how much we love *(pet's name)*
And now *(pet's name)* is not very well.
Please help us to look after *(pet's name),*
Help the vet to know how to treat *(pet's name)*
And, if possible, make *(pet's name)* better again.
Amen

Dear God,
Our pets are very special.
They give us love and many happy hours.
They teach us how to love and look after them.
They are our friends.
They let us know we're not alone.

So, when they die, we are sad inside.
Help us in our sadness to remember
all the good things about our pets
and to thank You for them.
Amen

Thank You for My Food

Thank You, God,
that I can break
my night-time fast
with breakfast.
What a great way
to start a day!
Amen

Munch, munch, munch,
Thank You for our lunch.

Dear God above,
For all Your love
and for our meal,
we thank You.

Thank You for my dinner;
Thank You for my friends;
Thank You for my family
And love that never ends.

For what we are about to receive,
May the Lord make us truly thankful.
Amen

Bless us, O Lord, and these Thy gifts,
Which of Thy bounty we are about to receive,
Through Christ our Lord.
Amen

I pray that ordinary bread
Be just as nice as cake;
I pray that I could fall asleep
As easy as I wake.

School lunches can taste nasty;
School lunches can taste nice.
But I love my school lunches;
I could eat them twice!

Some days, I eat up everything;
Sometimes, I like to share.
Thank You for school lunches, God,
Because my friends are there.

Pizzas and burgers; a plate of hot dogs;
Barbecued chicken that everyone hogs!

Candy and ice cream; a big birthday cake;
Gingerbread cookies that I helped to make.

These are the things that we all love to eat.
Thank You, dear Father, for each tasty treat.

Oh, the Lord is good to me,
And so I thank the Lord
For giving me the things I need,
The sun, the rain, and the apple seed.
Oh, the Lord is good to me.

JOHN "APPLESEED" CHAPMAN (1774–1845)

Cows make milk
And bees make honey.
Farmers cut corn
When it's sunny.
Plums and apples
Grow on trees.
And in Dad's garden
Are beans and peas.
Thank You, God,
For the food I eat,
For fruit and milk,
And bread and meat.
If it were not for
These gifts from You,
I really don't know what we'd do!

273

All this world is God's own field,
Fruit unto His praise to yield;
Wheat and tares together sown,
Unto joy or sorrow grown;
First the blade and then the ear,
Then the full corn shall appear:
Lord of the harvest, grant that we
Wholesome grain and pure may be.

HENRY ALFORD (1810–1871)

Red tomato,
Orange carrot,
Yellow pepper,
Lettuce green,
Beetroot that has blue and purple,
Indigo and violet sheen.
Thank You, God, that in my salad
Rainbow colors can be seen.

Here are the apples;
Here the pears,
Crusty bread,
And cream eclairs;
Potatoes and onions,
Barley and rye,
Honey in pots,
And rhubarb pie;
Berries and cherries
And bales of hay.
Thanks be for the harvest
God gave us today.

276

Father, we thank Thee for this food,
For health and strength and all things good.
May others all these blessings share,
And hearts be grateful everywhere.

Thank You, God,
For this day,
This family
And this food.
Amen

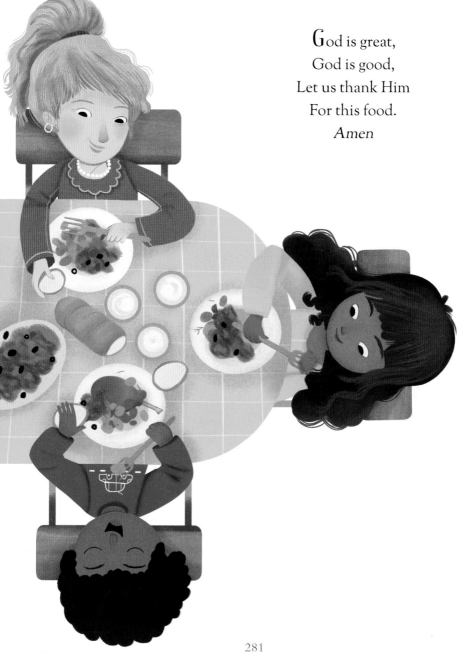

God is great,
God is good,
Let us thank Him
For this food.
Amen

Jesus fed the multitude
On five loaves and two fishes.
We don't know how He did it,
But, Jesus, bless these dishes!

Some hae meat and canna eat,
And some wad eat that want it;
But we hae meat and we can eat,
And sae the Lord be thankit.

ROBERT BURNS (1759–1796)

Thank You for the precious food
I eat three times a day.
Some children eat just once a week,
So, for them, I pray.
I wish that I could help them,
But I don't know what to do.
Please, God, will You make sure
That they have three meals, too?

283

May we who have much
Remember those who have little.

May we who are full
Remember those who are hungry.

May we who are loved
Remember those who are lonely.

May we who are safe
Remember those who are in danger.

May we who have so much
Learn to share.

Look After My Family

God bless all those that I love.
God bless all those that love me.
God bless all those that love those that I love,
And all those that love those that love me.

FROM AN OLD NEW ENGLAND SAMPLER

Jesus said,
"Let the little children come to me,
for the kingdom of God
belongs to such as these."

MATTHEW 19:14; MARK 10:14; LUKE 18:16

God bless you,
God bless me,
And keep us safe
As safe can be.

God bless Mom and Dad
For all the good times we have had;
For vacations, birthdays, Christmas fun;
For games and races that I won!

For afternoons spent in the park;
For watching fireworks after dark;
For all the stories they have read
At night, when I go up to bed.

Keep them safe, oh Lord, I pray,
So I can love them every day.

Once, I was a baby;
I used to wear a bib—
But now there's someone else
Sleeping in my crib!
Mom says it's my new brother.
He's very small and sweet,
With hands the size of daisies
And very smooth, pink feet.
I think I'm going to like him
And I know that he'll like me.
God, won't it be terrific
When I can hold him on my knee?

Look After My Family

We've got a new baby.
It's part of our family now.
When it holds my hand
and when it smiles at me,
I like it very much.

We've got a new baby.
It's hungry all the time.
When it makes a smell,
and cries and cries,
I don't like it at all.

Thank You for our new baby.
On bad days and good;
It's part of our family now
and I love it.

Lord, help us to remember that
Love is patient, love is kind.
It does not boast, it is not proud.
It is not envious or self-seeking.
It is not angry, but forgiving.
Love does not lie, but rejoices in truth.
It always protects, it always trusts.
It always hopes, it always tries.
Love never fails.

1 Corinthians 13

Dear God,
I do love my brother,
But I don't always like him.
Sometimes, we fight
And do mean things to each other.
Help me to remember that,
Even when I don't like him,
I still love him.
Amen

Dear God,
You won't be pleased
With what I did today.
My sister tried to kiss me,
But I turned my face away.
Please tell her that I love her
And I'm really going to try
To be a lot more loving,
But it's hard because I'm shy.

Thank You for Nan,
Who does what she can
When we go to her place.
Thank You for Grandpa,
Who knows where the candies are
And always says grace.
Thank You for visits
And all kinds of treats.
Thank You for walking
Down different streets.
Thank You for good times
Wherever we roam.
But most of all, God,
Thank You for home.

Peace be to this house
And to all who dwell here.
Peace be to those that enter
And to those that depart.

Grandma sits me on her knee,
Strokes my hair, and sings to me.

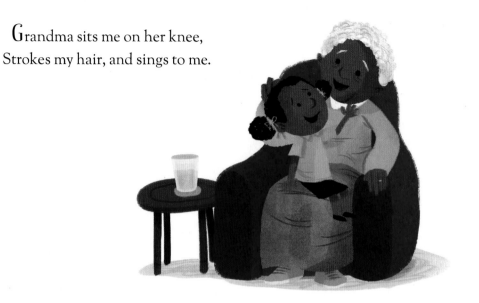

Grandpa jokes and plays baseball,
And picks me up when I fall.

At lunchtime, Grandpa likes to cook,
While Grandma sits and reads a book.
I love them, Lord, and pray that they
Will be there for me every day.

Dear God,
I kept a caterpillar in a jar
And it went into a little black cocoon.
I thought it was dead.
But, later, out of the cocoon
Came a beautiful butterfly.
Help me to remember
That people who die
Are a bit like my caterpillar.
In Your home in heaven,
They will be happy again,
Like beautiful butterflies.
Amen

Dear God,
If You are listening,
My granny died last night.
Mom says she's gone to heaven
And Dad said, "Yes, that's right."
So, God, if You should see her
In heaven up on high,
Tell her I shall miss her
And I'm sad to say goodbye.

Dear God,
Thank You for my family
and the things we do together.

Thank You for the meals we eat,
for the jokes we share,
for the bikes we ride,
and the place where we live.
Help us to remember
that we are part of Your family.

Look after my family
when we have to be apart.
Thank You for the thoughts we share,
the phone calls we make,
the memories we keep,
the prayers we pray.
Help us to remember
that You are with us all.
Amen

Help Me to Be Good

What can I give Him,
Poor as I am?
If I were a shepherd,
I would bring Him a lamb.
If I were a wise man,
I would do my part—
Yet what I can I give Him:
Give Him my heart.

CHRISTINA ROSSETTI (1830–1894)

Guide us, teach us, and strengthen us,
O Lord, we beseech Thee,
Until we become such as Thou would'st have us be:
Pure, gentle, truthful, high-minded,
Courteous, generous, able, dutiful, and useful;
For Thy honor and glory.

CHARLES KINGSLEY (1819–1875)

Lord, teach me all that I should know;
In grace and wisdom I may grow;
The more I learn to do Thy will,
The better may I love Thee still.

ISAAC WATTS (1674–1748)

Day by day, dear Lord, of Thee
Three things I pray:
To see Thee more clearly,
To love Thee more dearly,
To follow Thee more nearly,
Day by day.

St. Richard of Chichester (1197–1253)

O God, make us children of quietness and heirs of peace.
Amen

St. Clement (First century)

Last night, when I went to sleep,
I prayed that You would help me keep
A promise that I made to Mom
Not to be so quarrelsome.

I've really tried so hard today
To keep the promise, come what may,
And, Jesus, You will never guess
I think I've managed, more or less!

Dear God,
I think I'll help more
And give my mom some pleasure.
I'll tidy up my bedroom
And be her "little treasure."

Do other children help much?
Please tell me if they do,
And I'll make a special effort
For Mom and Dad and You.

Dear God,
I'm going to really try
To be good as good all day
And nice to all my special friends
When I go out to play.
If they say nasty things to me,
I mustn't do the same.
I don't want Mom to tell me off,
Or worse—give me the blame!
But, God, it isn't easy
To be as nice as pie,
So I know that You will help me
To really, really try!

Jesus, may I walk Your way
(point to feet)

in all I do
(hold out hands)

and all I say.
(touch finger to lips)
Amen

This is me
Looking up at You.
Help me
Always be
Close to You.

Help me to notice
when people need a hand.
Help me to see when they are sad
and need a friend.

Keep me from being
too busy to see
when someone needs a little help
from someone like me.

Sometimes, I'm good,
but I can be bad.
Sometimes, I'm happy;
sometimes, I'm sad.

I can be helpful,
I can be mean.
Sometimes, I'm somewhere
in between.
Help me to do what I know I should do.
Help me to choose to be good like You.

Dear God,
Help me to be good
when I have to share my toys.
Help me to be good
when I'm making too much noise.
Help me to be good
and eat up all my greens.
Help me to be good
when I'm tempted to be mean.
Help me to be good
each and every day.
Help me to be good
in every single way.
Amen

Make me pure, Lord: thou art holy;
Make me meek, Lord: thou wert lowly.

GERARD MANLEY HOPKINS (1844–1889)

It's a Special Day

Our Father in heaven,
Hallowed be Your name.
Your kingdom come,
Your will be done,
On Earth as it is in heaven.
Give us today our daily bread,
And forgive us our sins,
As we forgive those who sin against us.
And lead us away from temptation
And deliver us from evil,
For Yours is the kingdom,
And the power, and the glory,
Forever and ever.
Amen

Christ be with me and within me;
Christ behind me;
Christ to win me;
Christ to comfort and restore me;
Christ beneath me;
Christ above me;
Christ in quiet and in danger;
Christ in hearts of all that love me;
Christ in mouth of friend and stranger.

St. Patrick (389–461)

332

Lord, be with us this day:
Within us to purify us;
Above us to draw us up;
Beneath us to sustain us;
Before us to lead us;
Behind us to restrain us;
Around us to protect us.

St. Patrick (389–461)

God be in my head,
And in my understanding;
God be in my eyes,
And in my looking;
God be in my mouth,
And in my speaking;
God be in my heart,
And in my thinking;
God be at my end,
And at my departing.

THE SARUM PRIMER

Let the words of my mouth,
and the meditation of my heart,
be acceptable in Thy sight, O Lord,
my strength, and my redeemer.

PSALM 19

Can I see another's woe,
And not be in sorrow, too?
Can I see another's grief,
And not seek for kind relief?

WILLIAM BLAKE (1757–1827)

Let us with a gladsome mind
Praise the Lord for He is kind;
For His mercies shall endure,
Ever faithful, ever sure.

JOHN MILTON (1608–1674)

Dear God,
This is Monday.
Help me to start a good week.
Amen

Dear God,
It's Tuesday.
It's still early in the week.
Be with me as I try to make it a good one.
Amen

Dear God,
Wednesday already!
Midway through the week.
Please bless all those I meet today.
Amen

Dear God,
Thank You for Thursday.
I've made a good start.
Please help me with the rest of the week.
Amen

Dear God,
It's Friday.
Nearly the weekend!
Time to look back on my week.
Thank You for being with me.
Amen

Dear God,
It's Saturday—yippeee!
So much to do; so little time.
Please bless all my friends today.
Amen

Dear God,
It's Sunday, Your day.
Happy day. Holy day.
Thank You for the week just gone.
Please help me to enjoy next week with You.
Amen

Sunday should be a fun day,
not a glum day.
Sunday should be a rest day,
not a work day.

When God finished making the world,
He had a rest, put up His feet,
And said, "That's good!"
Dear God, thank You for this Sunday.
Help us to rest and play,
To celebrate and say, "That's good!"

Today is a day to remember—
I finally pulled out my loose tooth!
I feel more grown up already.
Thank You, God, for special days to remember.
Amen

Here is the church,
(link hands)
Here is the steeple,
(put index fingers together)
Look inside,
*(keeping your hands linked,
turn them upside down)*
Here are the people!
(wiggle your fingers)

The things, good Lord, that we pray for,
give us grace to work for;
through Jesus Christ our Lord.

SIR THOMAS MORE (1478–1535)

These candles on my cake,
I blow them out,
A wish I make.
To this wish,
I add a prayer:
Please, God, be with me
Everywhere.

Dear Jesus,
Everyone thought you were dead.
They took you down from the cross, with tears in their eyes,
and buried you in a cave with a big stone outside.
Then they went home—the saddest people on Earth.

Later, they went back
to take flowers, but they got such a shock.
The stone was rolled away, the cave was empty,
and you were walking in the garden.
Then, they were the happiest people on Earth.
No wonder we are happy at Easter.
We know that you're alive
and always will be.

347

Happy birthday, Jesus!
Thank you for sharing your special day with us.
The wise men brought you gifts,
so we give presents.
Your family was happy,
and we have parties and food.
Thank you for giving us Christmas.
Happy birthday, Jesus!

We've been packing our stuff;
we've been counting the days;
we've been saying goodbye
in a whole lot of ways.
It's a very special day—we're moving!

Please travel with us
as we leave our old home.
Please help us to know
that we're never alone.

Now I'm Going to Sleep

Now the daylight goes away,
Savior, listen while I pray.
Asking Thee to watch and keep,
And to send me quiet sleep.

Jesus, Savior, wash away
All that has been wrong today:
Help me every day to be
Good and gentle, more like Thee.

REV. WILLIAM HENRY HAVERGAL (1793–1870)

When in the night I sleepless lie,
My soul with heavenly thoughts supply;
Let no ill dreams disturb my rest,
No powers of darkness me molest.

Praise God, from whom all blessings flow;
Praise Him all creatures here below,
Praise Him above, ye heavenly host;
Praise Father, Son and Holy Ghost.

BISHOP THOMAS KEN (1637–1711)

Matthew, Mark, Luke, and John,
Bless the bed that I lie on.
Four corners to my bed,
Four angels round my head,
One to watch and one to pray,
And two to bear my soul away.

God bless this house from roof to floor,
The twelve apostles guard the door;
Four angels to my bed;
Gabriel stands at the head,
John and Peter at the feet,
All to watch me while I sleep.

Hush! my dear, lie still and slumber,
Holy angels guard thy bed!
Heavenly blessings without number,
Gently falling on thy head.

Sleep, my babe; thy food and raiment,
House and home, thy friends provide;
All without thy care or payment,
All thy wants are well supplied.

How much better thou'rt attended
Than the Son of God could be,
When from heaven He descended
And became a child like thee!

Soft and easy is thy cradle:
Coarse and hard thy Savior lay:
When His birthplace was a stable,
And His softest bed was hay.

Isaac Watts (1674–1748)

Ah, dearest Jesus, holy child,
Make thee a bed, soft, undefiled
Within my heart, that it may be
A quiet chamber kept for thee.

MARTIN LUTHER (1483–1546)

I see the Moon,
And the Moon sees me;
God bless the Moon,
And God bless me.

Gentle Jesus, hear me,
Will you please be near me?
I don't want to be alone,
Feeling sad all on my own.
Tomorrow will be different
At the start of a new day,
But until the morning comes,
Stay close to me, I pray.

Dear God,
I'm staying over with my friend tonight,
We'll have a terrific time and not fight.
We'll eat too much; we'll laugh with glee.
So, when You come to look for me,
I won't be in my bed;
I'll be with my friend instead.

Day is done;
Gone the sun
From the lake,
From the hills,
From the sky.
Safely rest,
All is well!
God is nigh.

Sleep, my child, and peace attend thee,
All through the night;
Guardian angels God will send thee,
All through the night;

Soft the drowsy hours are creeping,
Hill and vale in slumber sleeping,
I, my loving vigil keeping,
All through the night.

TRADITIONAL WELSH PRAYER

Watch, O Lord,
with those who wake,
or watch or weep tonight,
and give your angels charge
over those who sleep.
Tend your sick ones,
O Lord Jesus Christ;
rest your weary ones;
bless your dying ones;
soothe your suffering ones;
pity your afflicted ones;
shield your joyous ones;
and all for your love's sake.

St. Augustine of Hippo (354–430)

Lord, keep us safe this night,
Secure from all our fears;
May angels guard us while we sleep,
Till morning light appears.

JOHN LELAND (1754–1841)

Now I lay me down to sleep,
I pray Thee, Lord, Thy child to keep:
Thy love guard me through the night
And wake me with the morning light.

Jesus, please be near me as I lie in bed tonight:
There's a dark place in the corner, and it's giving me a fright!
Mom says it's just a shadow, and shadows are thin air,
But I can see it grinning, and it's sitting in my chair!
Please shine your light, dear Jesus, so that I can see
The shadow's really nothing now you are close to me.

When I put my hands together,
When I say a prayer,
When I stop and say Your name,
You are there.

When I'm frightened of the dark,
When I've had a scare,
When I think I'm all alone,
You are there.

I'm sleeping at my grandma's,
And I miss my mom and dad.
But Grandma cooked my favorite meal,
And now I'm not so sad!

I like to sleep at Grandma's;
She says it makes her glad.
Please, God, bless my grandma,
And bless my mom and dad.

It's time to sleep.
I've brushed my teeth
and read my book,
I've put my robe
on the hook,
and—

I just can't sleep.
The bed's too hot,
the light's too bright,
there's far too many
sounds tonight,
but—

I still can't sleep.
I've shut my eyes,
I've said a prayer,
"God bless children
everywhere,"
then—

Perhaps I'll sleep.
I think I might.
I think I'll—yawn—
turn out the light.
Goodnight.
Zzzzz ...

Good night! Good night!
Far flies the light;
But still God's love
Shall flame above,
Making all bright.
Good night! Good night!

VICTOR HUGO (1802–1885)

The Moon shines bright,
The stars give light
Before the break of day;
God bless you all
Both great and small
And send a joyful day.

Index of Prayers

Ah, dearest Jesus, holy child 359

All things bright and beautiful 202

All things praise Thee, Lord most high 219

All this world is God's own field 274

Beetles are funny 248

Bless us, O Lord, and these Thy gifts 265

Can I see another's woe 336

Christ be with me and within me 332

Cows make milk 273

Day by day, dear Lord, of Thee 314

Day is done 365

Dear Father, Hear and bless 247

Dear God above, For all Your love 263

Dear God, Bless our nets as we cast and trawl 206

Dear God, Help me to be good 326

Dear God, I do love my brother 298

Dear God, I kept a caterpillar in a jar 304

Dear God, I love to be on the beach 224

Dear God, I think I'll help more 317

Dear God, I'm going to really try.. 318

Dear God, I'm staying over 364

Dear God, If You are listening.. 305

Dear God, Our pets are very special.. 258

Dear God, Thank You for my family 306

Dear God, Thank You for the sun so bright............................. 214

Dear God, This is Monday.. 338

Dear God, You won't be pleased 299

Dear Jesus, Everyone thought..347

Father, we thank Thee for this food...279

For air and sunshine, pure and sweet......................................209

For all the rich autumnal glories spread..................................216

For flowers that bloom about our feet.....................................208

For this new morning and its light 212

For what we are about to receive 265

Gentle Jesus, hear me 362

God be in my head..335

God bless all those that I love 288

God bless Mom and Dad.. 290

God bless our school 230

God bless the animals.. 255

God bless the field and bless the furrow 221

God bless this house.. 357

God bless you... 288

God is great 281

God made the world so broad and grand............................ 212

Good night! Good night! 376

Grandma sits me on her knee 302

Guide us, teach us, and strengthen us 312

Happy birthday, Jesus! 348

He prayeth best, who loveth best... 247

Help me to notice.. 322

Here are the apples 276

Here is the church.. 343

Hurt no living thing... 246

Hush! my dear, lie still and slumber 358

I have quiet friends 231

I love to see the raindrops 228

I pray that ordinary bread 265

I see the Moon...360

I'm sleeping at my grandma's 373

It's time to sleep 374

Jesus fed the multitude 282

Jesus said...288

Jesus, may I walk your way 320

Jesus, our brother, strong and good... 236

Jesus, please be near me 370

Josie is my best friend 222

Joy to the world!.. 218

Last night, when I went to sleep 316

Let the words of my mouth.. 336

Let us with a gladsome mind 337

Little lamb, who made thee?...244

Lord, be with us this day 333
Lord, help us to remember that 296
Lord, keep us safe this night 369
Lord, teach me all that I should know.................................. 312
Loving Shepherd of Thy sheep 251
Make me pure, Lord 327
Matthew, Mark, Luke, and John 357
May we who have much 284
Munch, munch, munch.. 262
Now I lay me down to sleep 369
Now the daylight goes away.. 354
O God, make us children of quietness...................................315
O, thought I! 217
Oh, the Lord is good to me 270
Once, I was a baby 292
Our Father in heaven 331
Peace be to this house.. 301
Pizzas and burgers.. 268

Please, God, You know how much we love.................................. 257

Please listen to this special prayer 256

Praise the Lord! Ye heavens adore Him............................... 219

Red tomato.. 275

School dinners can taste nasty 267

Sleep, my child, and peace attend thee............................366

Some hae meat and canna eat.......................................283

Sometimes, I'm good 324

Sunday should be a fun day..340

Thank You for flowers...227

Thank You for my dinner 263

Thank You for Nan 300

Thank You for the precious food 283

Thank You, God, for giving us................................... 240

Thank You, God, for showing me 205

Thank You, God, For this day 280

Thank You, God, that I can break 262

The little cares that fretted me....................................243

The Moon shines bright..377

The things, good Lord, that we pray for 344

The year's at the spring 215

These candles on my cake 344

This is me 321

To all the humble beasts there be 252

Today is a day to remember 342

Tomorrow is a special day 210

Watch, O Lord, with those who wake 368

We've been packing our stuff.................................351

We've got a new baby 293

What can I give Him...310

When dogs bark and hamsters squeak 250

When I put my hands together...............................371

When I travel in a bus 232

When in the night I sleepless lie............................355

Wide as the world 229